D0800445

California

CALIFORNIA

Jennifer Denrow

FOUR WAY BOOKS
TRIBECA

Copyright © 2011 by Jennifer Denrow
No part of this book may be used or reproduced in any manner
without written permission except in the case of brief quotations
embodied in critical articles and reviews.

Please direct all inquiries to:
Editorial Office
Four Way Books
POB 535, Village Station
New York, NY 10014
www.fourwaybooks.com

Library of Congress Cataloging-in-Publication Data

Denrow, Jennifer.
  California / Jennifer Denrow.
      p. cm.
  ISBN 978-1-935536-08-6 (pbk. : alk. paper)
  I. Title.
  PS3604.E587C35 2011
  811'.6--dc22

                        2010032296

This book is manufactured in the United States of America
and printed on acid-free paper.

Four Way Books is a not-for-profit literary press. We are grateful for the assistance
we receive from individual donors, public arts agencies, and private foundations.

This publication is made possible with public funds
from the National Endowment for the Arts

and from the New York State Council on the Arts, a state agency.

Distributed by University Press of New England
One Court Street, Lebanon, NH 03766

[clmp] We are a proud member
of the Council of Literary Magazines and Presses.

for Michael Glen

CONTENTS

How the mind works still to be sure

Samuel Beckett

You were the white field when you handed me a blank
sheet of paper and said you'd worked so hard
all day and this was the best field you could manage.
And when I didn't understand, you turned it over
and showed me how the field had bled through,
and then you took out your notebook and said how each
time you attempted to make something else, it turned out
to be the same field. You worried that everyone
you knew was becoming the field and you couldn't help
them because you were the one making them into fields
in the first place. It's not what you meant to happen.
You handed me a box of notebooks and left. I hung the field
all over the house. Now, when people come over, they think
they're lost and when I tell them they're not, they say they're
beginning to feel like the field and it's hard because they know
they shouldn't but they do and then they start to grow whiter
and whiter and then they disappear. With everyone turning
into fields, it's hard to know anything. With everyone turning
into fields, it's hard to be abstract. And since I'm mostly alone,
I just keep running my hand over the field, waiting.

ACT 1

California

Forget your life.

Okay, I have.

Lay something down that is unlike you:

Sold boat, Italian song.

I'm losing my head over this:

this is what the doll said when you pulled its head
from its body;

all the girls laughed.

I'll move to California. I should
go alone. I'll go

with the knowledge of fake
snow. I'll ask my father to bring me.

I liked it better
when my fingers
were people.

I should drive away from my life.

If a man comes through town on his way to California, I will go with
him. I don't care who he is:

if his wife is pretty, fine;
if he is returning to her, fine.

A man should be going there today,

at least one man; this city
is so big.

When I'm in California I'll go to the beach
and cry. All of the seagulls will crowd

around me and force my mouth open
with their wings. One

will bring me a fish. I won't be able to leave them.

My fingers
aren't people
anymore.

I forgot to train them. They were over-watered. They drowned.

There isn't a steeple, no alderman
discussing the loss. That was a hand-church;

that was my folly.

My life in California will be inspiring. I'll send postcards to people who didn't know I was going. I'll even send postcards to people I haven't talked to in years.

I'll buy a guitar once I arrive.

I'll audition at a local club to become the nightly entertainment.

I'll say, *I can do anything you need.*

I'll show them card tricks and how my dog can talk.

I won't have a dog.

Everyone will laugh at me.

When it's winter and the woman next door needs to borrow some change for laundry, I'll call someone and say how unhappy I am.

I shouldn't go to California then.

No one can be alive there.

The store windows are just so the owners think people are alive.

I've never even wanted to go to California before.

I should leave now.

I went to wake up my husband to tell him I was leaving. He said, *Why do you want to go there?*

Because I have to.

You should fly then.

He won't let me borrow his car.

My car doesn't work.

I know a guy who should be driving to California this week. I check my email to see if he has written to ask me to go along.

He hasn't.

The computer says the right person is out there waiting for me. It asks for my name and age. I told my husband to make a profile on a love match website and I would do the same and we could see if we are compatible. He doesn't want to, so instead I ask if I can talk in his mouth and he lets me but says it tickles.

Later when he wakes up he'll say, *What was all of that about California?*

And I'll say, *Oh nothing.*

And he'll say, *You're pushing me away.*

And I'll say, *Probably, but I don't mean to.*

He'll leave for work and I'll spend the day listening to my favorite musician sing very sad songs that will make me want to go far away from myself.

I'll go to California then.

When I went to the backyard,

I said to myself,

this doesn't look like California

and nothing in my life does

and my husband says he'll have to deal with this forever.

I want to go so bad I clench my fist
hard in the air, I push my finger into
his chin and cry: *It feels like this*, I say,
I need it this bad.

I realize now that I'm a woman.

I go to the store.

I buy California style pizza and beer. I drop my ID when the woman asks to see it.

No one in the store looks like they could be from California.

A baby eats some keys.

I buy a magazine with people from California in it; they are all very beautiful.

I come out of the store and the sky
is filled with many white clouds

that could be stand-ins for California clouds.

I don't even have a tan.

I know this is the only time I'll leave the house today.

When I get home my husband sees me balling my fist and he scowls at me. On the radio is a story about a woman who walked from California to New York. She was 80. She says we don't have a democracy.

I need to arrive at something.

Now there is a story about a thirteen-year-old boy who is dying. He tells the reporter not to sit around being miserable. He gasps for breath.

He won't ever be able to dive into a pool.

He is a beautiful child.

He is dead.

He told the reporter to always let someone in line in front of him.

The next story is about the unibomber's brother. His mother kissed his cheek when he told her about her son.

She said, *I can't imagine what you've been going through.*

If I was in California, I wouldn't be listening to the radio.

I write California in the air.

Another story comes on about a man who built a cork boat.

I bring up images of California on the computer; there are three million to choose from. I set one as the screen saver. It's a yellow map of the southern part.

Instead of going to California I make my husband a ham and cheese sandwich to take to work. He doesn't like the way I place the cheese on the bread.

When he leaves for work I sit in a quiet house.

I told him I couldn't have this life.

This wasn't me living here.

I was living in California.

He said cruel things about having me committed.

He brought the ring from the cabinet and tried to put it on my finger.

I said no.

I said I can't be married right now.

He said this happens every year.

My mother took me to California once when I was very small. We visited Disneyland. I wore Mickey Mouse ears and had my hair in braids.

I wasn't afraid. No one talked to me.

On the plane ride home the stewardess offered us soft drinks.

Once on a plane a foreign woman offered me fruit.

I declined.

This was when I was older, after I'd already been to California.

When I was there, I wrote my name in the sand. I wrote my name and drew a heart and then I wrote my mother's name. This was when she loved my father so I wrote his name, too.

We were visiting my uncle.

I see a picture of him holding me and laughing.

He's dead now, so I can't visit him there anymore.

He had diabetes and drank a lot and died alone in a motel room.

My aunt said she received a phone call from him after he was dead. He groaned a little and said unintelligible things.

He lived in California because he was in the Navy and had to live there.

If I lived in California, I would buy an iguana. I would meet a lot of nice people. They would make kind remarks about the decision to follow my intuition.

Leonard Cohen went to California.

He went there to become holy.

I could become holy in California. I could live in a small room with only a little light.

My husband says I can rent a car if I really need to go. I tell him it's not the same. Why doesn't he ever feel something like this? He just doesn't.

He lives in this house completely.

This house could be the problem.

I suspect that I'm the problem.

He says I want to abandon our animals; he says I'm crazy.

I don't feel like I'm crazy,

I just feel like someone who wants to go to California.

I just remembered that I know someone who lives in California. He's a man I worked with several years ago. He moved there to make movies.

We made a movie once. It was a horror film that took place in a movie theatre. We worked in a movie theatre.

Our dialogue was poor.

I finally gave up.

I fell in love with the manager. We had sex. We laughed the whole time.

This was the first time I had sex. I was twenty-two. He didn't love me.

Later, I realized that I never really loved him either, I just pretended to so I could be sad about something. He was very charming and said funny things. He never took his hat off because he was going bald and didn't want anyone to know. His girlfriend was very sweet. He made all of the girls love him. Even the prettiest Mormon girl loved him. I started doing a lot of heroin then so it didn't matter that she loved him. I saw them kiss and felt nothing.

He is the kind of man who could live in California.

He had a very fast car and a lot of male friends.

If he lived in California, he might be a politician.

On the television I saw the President in a fast food restaurant in California. He was buying a cup of coffee for a reporter. Someone went to get the coffee, a recently new citizen, and when he came back and tried to hand it to the reporter, the President pushed his arm away and said, *I'll handle that*. He took the coffee from the new citizen and handed it to the reporter himself, and then he took some folded ones from his pocket and handed them back to the citizen.

He was trying to be real.

He was trying to look like the kind of person who wanted to be in California.

If California didn't exist, I'd still want to go there.

As I look around the house I think of things I'll take with me.

I pack my bags.

Before my husband left he asked if I would be here when he got home.

Yes.

But you'll be gone someday.

Yes.

Will you at least leave a note?

Yes.

The last man I left got a note. I didn't leave him for California but for my husband.

He was an angry man anyways. The note I left was filled with a lot of things about aggression and happiness.

After I left, he went to California for an art show. He married his ex-girlfriend. I knew he loved her the whole time he loved me. I didn't talk about her. I let him have her in silence.

My cousin calls. She tells me there are only 363 days until the new Harry Potter movie comes out. My aunt gets on the phone. I tell her about California. She tells me about a man who lost his leg but can still feel two toes fall asleep.

The reality is that . . .

My aunt talks like this.

She says his leg is not really gone. That's not reality. She tells me how Christ replaced someone's ear.

I hear her daughter in the background asking to borrow some pot. *Here, but make it last, I don't want to go back over there in two days,* my aunt says. Back over there is to the house of the man with one leg and phantom toes.

When I was a teenager my mom would put extra pot on a cheese plate that had a mouse cover. She would say, *it's there in case you need to relax.* I didn't need to relax but I still took the pot. When my friends came over I said we had to smoke in the garage. This was a lie. I don't know why I said this.

My aunt says California is a little far, but she could pick me up in a few days and we could go to Chicago.

I am suddenly terrified to leave the house, but I tell her that will be fine.

She probably won't come. She usually forgets to do things like that, so I don't worry too much.

We talk for two hours. She tells me how frustrating it is to get laid off three times in four years.

She applies for nine jobs a week.

No one calls her back.

She says perhaps if she was in California it would be easier to get a job.

The living room's dark now.

The streetlight comes through the window like a forgotten angel.

By this time it's apparent that I'm not leaving for California today.

I should go to sleep.

I'll leave tomorrow.

Maybe I'll meet someone who's going there.

They'll casually mention it and I'll say I was thinking about going there myself.

ACT 2

Things Reappear

Because the chair in front of you
isn't a base, you don't touch
it when you pass by.

The other players foul you for this.

Your scorecard is empty.

You put your thumb in front of your eye.

This is the world now.

The Understudy

She knew your lines
so much better than you knew them.
You asked to trade with her but she said
no. She said these were your lines
even if you didn't know them,
even if someone different from yourself
knew them and said them all of the time.
She broke character to tell you this.
You felt bad then.

OPENING NIGHT

I carry the director into another
room and shut the houselights off.

The Doctor's Office

You can explain everything
to me and then I can explain
it to you and we can see
the difference. When the nurse
calls my name, I won't answer.

DEAR DECK,

Haven't the nails been enough?

You could be a lot of things moving, or worse,

You could be the last girl with a crayon bank.

This is just the sky that keeps happening.

One person you love talks about horses, and you're glad you don't have to become one—

Even so, arms at your sides, you agree to be looked at.

The Hairdresser

I touch the hairdresser to make sure I have hair.
Scissors can rescue nothing.
The hairdresser believes in them.
I touch her again to believe in her.
Her eyes are made of scissors. She cries hair.
She knits while she cuts my hair.
We talk about passengers, the importance of remaining calm for them.
I am her best passenger.
I touch her mouth to be sure.

After It's Gone

See how there's
nothing. If you put a magician out here,
he'd disappear. As the sky mentions
the mountains, it recedes.
I know because I keep
seeing it even though I don't mean to.
I tell the birds
how it's all a mistake.
They fly into me and then struggle
to leave.

DIAGRAMS OF ANIMALS

Most of the time, waking.
All sky. Beside yourself,
someone who resembles
leaving. You imagine
you will stand like a sheriff
and if this fails, you will
stand like a clerk.

Sometimes, wind.
Sometimes, wind and you can hear it
going through you.

IF REFLECTION

You can put anything in the sky.

You can put yourself in the sky.

And if that doesn't work,

You can use a bird.

There is so much to the world.

Stop taking apart the sky.

I can't.

When I tell people about the sky

They say, yes, we know.

In Defense of Everything

—after Peter Gizzi

The sky will never do
and that common crow, struggling against it, won't work either.
The snow says, *You keep giving me angels I didn't ask for.*
It seems your bodies are for nothing but making angels.
The past is how you walked over to yourself, laughing.
This is what you have guessed at—
things get bigger: after the sky, the sky,
and after that, the flecked lark
beating himself up.

You vs.

When you showed someone your badge,
they said it wasn't real and unclipped it.
You no longer thought of yourself as
an active member of the police force.

Your Character

Sometimes, when the wind comes like that,
and the trees struggle to be trees,
you try to be like them. You draw a black hole
on your stomach. You think that the beginning
of being a tree must be so hard. Your arms
tire quickly.

CONTACTED TREE. EMPTY ROAD. WAITED EVENING.

Don't worry.
If you're not fond
of the sky, there isn't one.
In theory, we are likely trading
it for the idea of falling.

MEMORIZATION

What goes on living:

the crow, the crow,
the tree. I make notes
to myself of their pleasures:

    water, yes,
    and ground.

They are like talking to nothing.

ACT 3

A Knee for a Life

The stones—who would believe it, had we not
The unimpeachable witness of Tradition?—
Began to lose their hardness, to soften, slowly,
To take on form, to grow in size, a little,
Become less rough, to look like human beings,
Or anyway as much like human beings
As statues do, when the sculptor is only starting,
Images half blocked out.

—Ovid's *Metamorphoses*

On the one hand, there is a gay, irrepressible Charlie, through whom, by some strange alchemy, the shy and pallid Bergen is transformed into a brilliant comedian. On the other hand, there is an imperious and dominating Charlie, whose almost-human personality has so eclipsed his creator that Bergen cannot function as an artist alone.

—New York Herald Tribune

Dear Edgar,

Even in the stage light
your birds are not quiet.

Your hand is a little colder today. Are you feeling well?

Has anyone ever told you your hands are like soft, skyless
animals? I am beginning to understand

why you chose this place: even the prisoners sing.

Yours,

Charlie

The show was crying, the audience calm.

Dear Charlie,

I only shut your case [discarnate, custodial] because of the draft.
Darkness is what happens sometimes.

I'll be planting most of the day; the violets
wait for me like strangers.

Call if you need me.

Love,

Edgar

Dear Edgar,

The salesman is a place I go often.

Even in this dark case I can still feel your hand. [never has their laughter hurt more]

And what after? Someone,
maybe a sad wife,

will want me. Don't let them take me to a museum. I can't breathe thinking of it.

Yours,

Charlie

Dear Charlie,

I watch the birds at the window; they last
so short a time.

They are growing less eager about the trees.

They have even perched on a branch for the better part of an hour,
flocking where other things break. [accordingly]

The rain piles like cold fish. The trees grow
needlessly on.

Don't worry. You won't go with me. [no one can love you more than I]

I am feeling a little better today.

Love,

Edgar

Dear Edgar,

You mention the sky, relentless
with clouds. The brief
light.

Last night I dreamt of a river. [it isn't the kind of thing you keep]

Pairs of women stood in the middle with their bodies
bent to make airplanes.

Does this mean you'll be gone soon?

Yours,

Charlie

"The eyes in all the heads stared dead and dark, the many faces lifeless. Because, after all, he needed my father for that part. Because he was nothing without my father."

—Candice Bergen

Dear Charlie,

This isn't the first time
you were afraid:

when you were small, the audience was angry with you for saying
breast instead of breath. Someone threw their coffee. You became so
terrified it took weeks before you would try it again.

[your often heart beats more competitively] Don't you remember?

Fear is like anything else; even in the morning it comes.

Love,

Edgar

Dear Edgar,

That's the fortuneteller's water. [light was in question, not fear] Last night my liner broke.

Goose feathers poking my arms.

Nothing inside the house will speak to me. Objects grow more strange each day.

Yours,

Charlie

Dear Charlie,

Even the quiet bird has given up silence. [think of Vegas]

I'm not sure I can help you.

Does anyone ever call you Edgar? Sometimes

they call me Charlie just to be cruel.

Love,

Edgar

"Charlie's head was carved by a Chicago wood-carver. If you are skilled with the wood-carving knives, you, too, can construct an excellent and natural-looking head."

—Edgar Bergen

Dear Edgar,

The wood-carver used to say terrible things;

I remember him often:

his suffix,

his grasp.

You've forgotten
my top hat all week.

I think you need to see someone. [I want to be a detective again]

Yours,

Charlie

Dear Edgar,

The trees only suffer

because you look at them.

I have loved you too often.

Nothing can relieve me.

Fall, in its lean way,

is back,

just to show me the face I'm left with;

your many hands.

Charlie

I put you away

Dear Edgar [this is insensitive],

The nights last for so long that I've stopped announcing the hours. I'm a man now, yet you treat me like a child. Just take me back to my room. Or don't. I could do the act alone; it's me they love. You're just a salesman, an impossible weight, and every time you touch me you give me a fever. I quit. You're walking so lunge-like now, you can barely hold yourself up; even the birds are concerned. One went for three days without water. He cussed when I saw him—he cussed and said you'd stolen his name from another show-bird, one with a failing musculature.

Dear [there are not enough answers] Charlie,

I dreamt that the microphone was full of throats

all calling to you,

your slim neck

craning toward me.

Love,

Edgar

P.S. I'm having your portrait done tomorrow.

Dear Charlie,

The Dr. is saying it. In fact,

he said it plainly: arthritis,

then patted my shoulder like I was a child.

Love,

Ed [I am long-hearted now] gar

Dear Edgar,

If I said I wasn't fond

of this body,

would you change it?

I'm terrified of leaving [a little more tugging of the curtain] the trunk.
Even the child's voice from across the street is frightening: she is
yelling about ponies, their off-white fur.

Can't you fix her mouth?

Yours,

Charlie

the teeth may be merely suggested

Dear Charlie,

I've known you since I was young, my body
gravid with sorrow.

We were boys for so long. A hand passes through
wood. Splinters.

Closet: a child turning on the light: your numberless bodies
hang like fresh suits.

We were young together in the worst way.

Love,

Edgar

"There was no one with him but his larynx."

—Candice Bergen

Dear Edgar,

[accordingly] You're not making sense.

Thank you for attempting clouds in my case, but I doubt I'll ever be
convinced.

Even in the dark I am like you. Pattern the sky
with more flight.

The empty post calling out to the birds, fat as comedians
and half as troubled.

Practice this: A E I O U.

You're allowed to move your lips. I will teach you
to become human:

Try: Thursday.

Try: I like land, when land lakes itself around lambs.

Try: I love you even though your back is flesh.

Yours,

Charlie

[this is my afterlife body]

Dear Charlie,

Lamb-quiet.

I get sores when I move [hemic] my lips. Your lessons are ridiculous.

If you go back to your case, I will let you cut your own pattern from the sky and I will stitch it to the velvet myself.

Love,

Edgar

you brought it up

Dear Edgar,

I'm sure you feel sad sometimes at the doll store.

I am *a very simply constructed doll.*

My hollow neck-stick perched
on by so many
[you get shadowgraphs for your life] sad birds.

It becomes more difficult,

the sky,

each time you look at it.

Love,

Charlie

Dear Charlie,

Your assemblage was nothing ordinary.

At the doll store, yes. The eyes
are fine things.

I have enough

life

for them all;

you always question that.

I cannot free anything. Someone told me
yesterday that they mistook my thoughts

for levers,

for lovers. They kept asking to see me again.
Even the sky, coughing its breaths,
began asking for me to shut its case.

[*mowed down*] Yours,

Edgar

"Stepping back from Charlie, I checked his appearance: The familiar brown eyes that for fifty years had shot sparks and flickered famously now stared past me stonily into space, strangely dull, glassy, dead. There was no sign of life; worse, no recognition. *Hey! It's me, Charlie, it's Candy*! I waited for the wisecracks that would never come, the throaty chuckle, the clipped movements. I was shocked at his final silence."

—Candice Bergen

Dear Edgar,

My mouth is somewhat damaged,
somewhat strange,

and my teeth are so crowded with other teeth
that I could never say the right thing.

[hesitantly] I met with the carpenter. We worked on your case all
day. We used pine and yellow velvet for the lining. If this isn't what
you expected, I'm sorry. Even the carpenter said it was time. Don't
worry that all of your shirts are backless; the tailor says you will look
handsome no matter what.

Love,

Charlie

anything but velvet

Dear Charlie,

I have said nothing.

Forgive [my bones are too big for you] me; the shallow

end empty of birds, nothing but bone spokes
and wind; no one coughing back anything.

Yours,

Edgar

Dear Edgar,

[bitterly] I am taking your plane.

I always knew you had it better than I did but you were
so convincing.

As for your birds, I [you need to stay in the case for
winter] let them go; they were so loud, how could you
stand it? Please don't be afraid. If you close your eyes
long enough, light starts to happen.

Love,

Charlie

Dear Char [echolalia is what you have, but no one has wanted to tell you] lie,

Hand over hand, we press the sky.

More of the same.

The lining is too thin. A E I O U.

Skinnier necks than most, but still crowded around each other: fish scales.

A E I O U.

Pedestrian, cover your heart, I can't walk to you.

AEIOU.

I wasn't trained for conclusions. I have come to know each pause. The sky unmanageable.

For my life, I get eggshells. Don't talk in the mirror for long. Throw your voice away. Only part your lips enough for company. Rope slack hanging from the sky,

the sky asking someone to pull.

[deliberately] Yours,

Edgar

ACKNOWLEDGEMENTS

Many thousands of thanks to Jay Thompson and *Thermos* for including "California" and Jen Tynes of Horse Less Press for putting together *A Knee for a Life*. Thank you to MARY for having "The Doctor's Office" and "Things Reappear."

All my love and thanks to everyone at Four Way Books, especially Ryan, who made this take place and made California real, and Martha for being so amazing and letting this happen, Thank you, thank you.

Thanks to Pont St. Cloud for always having the ocean in her eyes and Tamara and Bre La La for being lights. Thank you to all my teachers and friends who continue to inspire me and help me be a person— these people are: Julie Adams, Rhiannon Dickerson, DeAnn Neeley, Maggie McDermott, Donna Denrow, Carrie White, Don Boone, Kevin Prufer, Wayne Miller, Kerri Webster, Mary Jo Bang, TaraShea Nesbit, Emily Winecke, Rachel Epstein, Alex Quinlan, Vincent Guerra, Eleni Sikelianos, Bin Ramke, and everyone in the very long list of workshops I've had for their patience and generosity, especially Arda, Jen and Jules for their undying availability and help in answering so many questions.

Thank you, Mom, for being made of compassion. And thank you, Dad, for your willingness to experience, with such dexterity, what's unfamiliar.

This book is for Michael Glen because he makes everything what it is.

West Tisbury Free Public Library

0 7000 0200599 4

Jennifer Denrow is the author of two chapbooks: *A Knee for a Life* (Horse Less Press, 2010) & *From California, On* (Brave Men Press, 2010). She currently lives in Colorado and is pursuing a Ph.D. at the University of Denver.

LL

DATE DUE MAR 0 7 2011

APR 1 6 2011

AUG 0 1 2011
SEP 0 8 2011